BAT REMODELING SECRETS

A Unique Guide To Cost-Effective Bathroom Remodeling From A 30-Year Bathroom Remodeler

TOM DEWELL

BRIGHTRAY
PUBLISHING®

We help busy professionals write and publish their stories
to distinguish themselves and their brands.

(407) 287-5700 | Winter Park, FL
info@BrightRay.com | www.BrightRay.com

ISBN: 978-1-956464-29-0

Published in the United States of America.
BrightRay Publishing ® 2023

TABLE OF CONTENTS

CHAPTER EIGHT: MIRRORS

CHAPTER NINE: BATHROOM LIGHTNING

CHAPTER TEN: SHOWER DOORS

To my parents, Jim and Barbara Dewell who, when I was a kid, never stopped me from making a mess in the garage as I built countless bikes, go-karts, and forts, all of which helped shape the direction of my future career in remodeling.

To my friends and partners, Brett, Scott, and Dan, with whom my remodeling journey started and with whom I had some of the best times of my career.

Thank you to my wife, Trish, and my kids, Kennedy, Gavin, and Graydin, for their patience and understanding of all the long days and nights of being away working on projects and completing jobs.

And thank you to all my employees, customers, and vendors. Without their hard work, support, and loyalty, I would not have had the privilege of being able to write this book.

INTRODUCTION

The inventory of older homes throughout the United States skews the ability to determine a definitive average bathroom size. U.S. home sizes have doubled since the 1950s, and newer homes typically have larger bathrooms on average than homes built pre-1980. For the sake of this book, we will consider an average bathroom to be 45 square feet laid out as a 5' x 9' blueprint. This would be typical of most one, two, and three-bedroom tract homes built in the 1950s through the 1990s. In other words, the bathroom has become more important, and every aspect of it needs to be cohesive. The balance between quality and affordability is key.

Each chapter in this book gives you information about a specific part or fixture in the bathroom. If you're planning a bathroom remodel, whether for the whole room or specific fixtures, you can easily go to the table of contents and find the chapter heading for the item you need. If you're reading this as an eBook, it's even easier; just click on the link, and you'll jump to that specific chapter.

This book is designed to take the national average cost of remodeling a bathroom and reduce the overall cost. I will show you ways to take up to 50% off the national average prices by teaching you tricks of the trade I've learned over three decades of experience as a remodeler.

The ideas and concepts of low-cost remodeling don't change a whole lot year to year, but pricing does. Additionally, depending on where you live, costs will greatly vary. I recommend you do local research prior to your remodel to get current pricing information for your market. I really don't care what the national average is; what's more important to me is the local average as well as how much remodeling vendors with good reviews are charging for the work that's needed.

This isn't written to be a do-it-yourself book. It's intended to help show where you can take shortcuts as well as places where shortcuts should never be taken. No matter the case, I'll teach you ways to reuse, refinish, or repurpose any fixtures you can. Every time you're able to keep current fixtures, you'll save money on your remodeling budget. I will steer you toward making quality-minded decisions in order to get the maximum value. If you've considered remodeling your bathroom, then this book is perfect for you.

USING THE WORD "FIXTURE"

In my main business of bathtub refinishing, we use the word "fixture," which encompasses most of the items I'll be talking about in later chapters. This includes bathtubs, showers, vanities, and countertops, among other things. I've never heard of a universal term to describe everything in a bathroom, including ceilings, floors, walls, and lighting. You could use "item" or "fixture," but for this book, I'm addressing anything built into your bathroom as a "fixture."

Before you decide to go ahead with the remodel, you should evaluate why you are remodeling. Is this your primary residence and you'd like a new bathroom? Are you flipping a house? Maybe you've just bought a house and need to do some updating. Maybe you're a real estate agent trying to determine if it makes sense for your client to do some bathroom updates.

Regardless of the reason, this book will help you make the absolute best decisions as you navigate through your project.

MY BACKGROUND

I've always been handy and interested in building things. As a kid, I was constantly taking things apart, curious as to how they worked, then trying to put them back together (which usually proved to be the toughest part). That interest in rebuilding things never left me.

Remodeling is a very gratifying profession—it provides me great satisfaction to remove or improve something that is old, worn, and ugly and turn it into something new, fresh, and beautiful.

In 1989, after a couple of years of playing college football for The College of San Mateo in the San Francisco Bay Area, I moved to San Diego to attend San Diego State University. It was during my time at SDSU that I really started my remodeling career. Working on the chapter house of my fraternity and various other houses that I rented while being a student gave me that gratifying feeling of fixing or improving something.

In 1992, at the age of 24, I graduated from college with a degree in business management. Unsure of what my future held for me, I spent some time in Orange County, California with some friends who had just started a bathtub refinishing business. They needed help on a large project at UC Irvine where they had recently graduated and were able to land a bathtub refinishing contract. I was looking for something to do, so it was a great fit that soon became a great partnership. I learned the trade of bathtub refinishing, which included repairing porcelain, fiberglass, laminate, cultured marble, tile, and really any bathroom material that could be refinished. I also learned how to remodel kitchens and bathrooms and eventually obtained a California "B" General Building Contractor license.

The ten-year partnership with my friends resulted in creating my own company in 2003 called Commercial Bath Refinishing (CBR), which is a full-service kitchen and bath refinishing company. Though CBR works mostly with multi-family housing and large property management companies providing refinishing services, I am still very drawn to larger-scale home remodeling.

As CBR grew to multiple locations throughout California and over 60 employees, I was fortunate to have the time and capital to simultaneously run my business and purchase real estate, eventually obtaining a California real estate license. During this time, I purchased, renovated, and sold over a dozen single-family homes for profit, learning many great lessons about how to effectively remodel for value and profit.

In all, I have been remodeling bathrooms for over thirty years now and have learned how to increase the value of a home on a shoestring budget. I have learned when you should keep and restore a fixture and when you should replace it. Most importantly, I have learned how to blend the two, using existing fixtures and mixing in some new items. I've learned how to produce a seamless, functional, and beautiful space for a fraction of the cost of the national average. Read on, and I assure you that if you have a bathroom remodel in your future, you will learn to create massive value and achieve the highest rate of return on your remodel while ending up with a room you love.

CHAPTER ONE

IS THERE A BATHROOM REMODEL IN YOUR FUTURE?

WHY YOUR BATHROOM COULD NEED REMODELING

Homeowners can have many reasons to want a bathroom upgrade. Many times, it's a matter of increasing the quality of their lives. If a family has an old, outdated bathroom with chipped, scratched, or worn-out fixtures, updating the areas that need attention will increase the family's satisfaction when using the room, otherwise known as the "joy" factor. According to the National Association of Realtors' 2022 Remodeling Impact Report, 84% of homeowners want to be in their homes longer after a remodeling project, 69% enjoy their homes more after a remodel, and 69% feel a major sense of accomplishment when they think about their completed project.[1]

However, aesthetics are not the only motivator for remodeling. Sometimes, it's a safety issue. Older porcelain bathtubs contain lead, and with chips and cracks, even small holes in the porcelain can cause health issues. Safety is a major concern for elderly or disabled people who are at a higher risk of slipping or falling while getting in or out of the bathtub or shower. Having those fixtures made safer with slip-resistant products, safety handles, or grab bars are all easy additions. Or, if entering the bathtub is not suited for someone's needs, a tub-to-shower conversion could be done, eliminating the need to step over the sidewall of a bathtub. This would be an easier and safer way for them to bathe since a shower allows easier entry.

Sometimes, a homeowner has no choice but to change a fixture. Maybe a bathtub or shower stall has a leak, and until it's repaired or replaced, it can't be used. Dripping faucets and plumbing leaks pose other problems which, when left unaddressed, could result in higher water bills or potential water damage leading to rot or mold.

Finally, you might want to upgrade your bathroom to add resale value. Bathroom remodels are a great way to add value to your home, especially when it comes to resale potential. Homebuyers like seeing updated bathrooms, so when you've put in the time and expense of making thoughtful upgrades, it often pays off in your sales price. There are lots of reasons people remodel bathrooms, and there are plenty of ways to do it.

THE COST OF REMODELING YOUR BATHROOM

When we look at the cost of remodeling a 45-square foot bathroom, it's easy to see why bathrooms are the most expensive room in your home per square foot. Your remodel costs will potentially be based on several different factors, including who you hire, the materials you select, and how much you want changed.

I mentioned earlier that I won't go into detail regarding national remodeling averages or specific pricing because it changes rapidly over time. However, I do want to touch on this to stress the point that the ideas and concepts provided in this book can create significant savings over traditional remodeling while still capitalizing on aesthetics, functionality, and a maximum return on investment. Therefore, we will quickly take a look at some of the national bathroom remodeling costs. *The Remodeling Magazine*'s 2022 Cost vs. Value report shows that a mid-range bathroom remodel generally costs about $27,000 but can climb to over $80,000 for an upscale or high-end larger bathroom remodel.[2]

A mid-range renovation includes materials like ceramic tile floors, new chrome fixtures, a ceramic tile surround, a single-lever shower handle, a standard white toilet, and a mid-grade vanity counter. The finishes are functional and nice but not top of the line. The national average cost for this type of remodel is over $27,000.

An upscale bathroom remodel may include structural changes like expanding or adjusting the layout. Finishes include things like large ceramic or stone floor tile, heated floors, high-end faucets, and natural stone countertops with double sinks. Showers may have heavy frameless glass doors, rain shower fixtures, shower niches, and tiled shower walls. Freestanding tubs are also found in this type of bathroom remodel. The national average cost for this type of remodel is over $80,000.

These costs may surprise you and might seem high, but keep in mind that these are for medium and high-end projects, which are not what this book was written for. Mid and high-range remodels involve replacing any old fixtures with new fixtures and completely renovating the space, not blending the old and new fixtures to maintain a budget. More in line with this book, the 2022 cost data from Home Advisor states that the average smaller bathroom remodel costs about $10,000 and that most homeowners spend between $6,000 to $15,000 on a bathroom project.[3]

Luckily, this book focuses on standard 5 x 9 bathrooms, which is what many of us have. The goal is to be able to renovate affordably with the knowledge of how to achieve quality results while staying well below the average national cost. A fresh, well-done, updated bathroom will get buyers' attention if you're selling and also bring joy to you during the time that you get to use the room as a homeowner. My methods keep it simple and inexpensive, keep the cost in the range of $3,000 to $7,000, provide the tips of the trade to keep you in line with whatever budget you have, and help you create a project you'll love and be proud of.

ROI ON A BATHROOM REMODEL

What kind of return on investment (ROI) is involved with a bathroom remodel? While no two bathroom renovations are exactly alike, they will almost always provide an increase in home value. Recognizing that every bathroom, home, and neighborhood differ, and remembering that many factors affect resale, it is generally agreed that bathrooms will provide the best ROI against price per square foot over any other room in the house. According to U.S. News, for example, investing in a bathroom remodel yields a 62% average ROI.[4]

A successful remodel means planning ahead and making good, thoughtful decisions about what upgrades you make, how many of the existing fixtures can be saved and reused, and choosing the latest trends in your product and service selections. As you will continue to see in the pages ahead, cosmetic changes tend to be smarter investments than major layout changes or overhauls. To get the most out of your bathroom remodel, focus on saving everywhere you can. If you are remodeling for resale, your real estate agent already knows that bathrooms are deal breakers (or makers) in a home sale, and buyers will place a premium on how much they like the bathrooms in a house they're looking to purchase.

Bathroom remodels won't necessarily return everything you spent to update it, but there is no question that it's one of the highest ROI projects you can do. A freshly remodeled bathroom also helps inspire offers on your house, and even small, inexpensive updates to this space could help bring the overall sales price on your home up 2-3%. Making educated remodeling decisions is the key, as everything you do—from deciding to replace the tub to restoring an old cabinet—is important to the bottom line.

It makes sense that ROI is naturally better when you spend less, so don't spend or replace when you don't have to. Start by focusing on what you don't like in the existing bathroom and what doesn't properly function. If you're considering the remodel for yourself, what is most important to you to have changed? If you're selling the home, what is going to look unsightly to a buyer during a home tour, or worse, on a home inspection report? Old paint on the walls (or an ugly color), cracked tiles, peeling caulking, water stains, and dirty grout are just a few items that are easy fixes which, when left unfixed, can turn a buyer away.

THE GOOD, BETTER, BEST SCENARIO

In many chapters of this book, I will discuss different options with fixtures. The "good, better, best scenario" helps explain these different options. "Good" means the lowest cost approach, "better" means a higher cost than "good" but still not going all out, and "best" typically means the highest cost approach. In all three scenarios, however, the "good" isn't necessarily the least favorable option; conversely, the "best" scenario isn't always the most advantageous approach. In fact, most of the time, the "good" or "better" options will be what I recommend, assuming we have a fixture that can be reused or repurposed. After all, if you can shave thousands of dollars off the cost of your remodel without jeopardizing quality or functionality, do it.

PERMITS

Depending on where you live and how extensive your remodel will be, you'll want to check with your local permit office to see if permits will be required. Every city or region has a governing body in charge of zoning, building codes, and regulations. Additionally, if you're using a contractor, they should be able to advise you if any permits will be needed for the work you're doing. Many remodeling items discussed in this book, however, will not require any special permits. Restoring or repairing a fixture will not require a permit, so doing any painting (including refinishing the bathtub, shower walls, or enclosures, as well as tile work) can normally be done without any permits. Installing plumbing valves or the addition of any electrical work may require a permit and need to be inspected to ensure the work conforms with local code.

CHAPTER TWO

BATHTUBS AND SHOWER BASES

We start the first appliance-specific chapter with bathtubs and shower bases for a few reasons. Not only is it near and dear to my heart since I've been in the bathtub refinishing business for over three decades, but also, including the next chapter (shower wet walls), these two fixtures combined can be by far the most expensive fixtures in the bathroom. Therefore, completing a full bathroom remodel on a budget has a lot to do with the decisions you make about your bathtub and shower enclosure.

Making good decisions as they relate to how you want to remodel your bathtub or shower pan requires some thought about what you really want to achieve both cosmetically and financially. When done correctly, choosing the right option for your bathtub or shower can greatly add to the beauty and functionality of your bathroom for years to come.

First, let's start with some terminology and history. Bathtubs and shower bases (pans) can be manufactured out of many material types. However, in most homes throughout the US, they are typically one of two main types, either porcelain or plastic. For porcelain, there is porcelain over cast iron or porcelain over pressed steel. For plastic, the options are either fiberglass or acrylic. Other less common materials include solid surface, cultured marble, tile, and stone. Shower bases are typically made of molded plastics, but I'm including both fixtures in this chapter since they are similar from a remodeling standpoint. If you have an older home dating from before the 1970s, there's a good chance that you have a porcelain tub in your home rather than a fiberglass or acrylic tub. Homes built from the turn of the 20th century and up to the mid-1960s typically had cast iron tubs, whereas tract builders of the late 1960s and early 1970s to current times have preferred either pressed steel porcelain tubs or one piece fiberglass or acrylic enclosures because of the low cost and ease of installation.

Let's take a look at the two most common materials used in bathtubs and shower bases, plastics and porcelain. Your bathroom most likely will have one of these two types. Plastic bathtubs and shower bases are made out of a number of different polymer materials, including ABS (acrylonitrile-butadiene-styrene), acrylic resins, or glass-fiber reinforced polyester.[5] The glass-polyester type dominates the modern-day tub-shower market.

FIBERGLASS

Also known as FRP, or fiberglass-reinforced plastic, this is typically going to be the least expensive bathtub and shower material. A fiberglass bathtub or shower pan is made by forming layers of fiberglass into the desired shape, then coating it with gelcoat resin. The advantages are that it's low cost, lightweight, easy to install, and has a finish that can be repaired. As for its downsides, fiberglass fixtures are thinner and able to flex, so the feeling under your feet is less stable. They tend to be less durable, and the finish is prone to fading, scratching, and cracking. However, they produce a warmer feel to the touch than porcelain and are popular because of the low cost.

ACRYLIC

Acrylic tubs use fiberglass sheets for reinforcement underneath vacuum-formed sheets of colored acrylic. The advantages are pretty much the same as with fiberglass, although acrylic tubs are more expensive and tend to be more durable. Like fiberglass, they also have a nice, warm feeling to the touch, unlike porcelain. The disadvantage is that the finish can scratch or discolor over time. You also have a lot of choices of shapes, sizes, and colors. Acrylic is an all-around good choice, although it may lack a certain high-end appeal for some homeowners.

PORCELAIN ENAMEL ON CAST IRON

Cast iron tubs are made by pouring molten iron into a mold of the desired shape after which dry enamel, which has been previously heated to a temperature above the melting point of enamel, is dusted on the metal surface. The powder melts on contact, forming a contiguous coating. Wet enamel may also be applied instead using automatic spraying equipment. Then, firing the tub in a furnace produces a smooth, porcelain-like surface. It's considered the most durable tub available, and the finish is the most resistant to chipping, scratching, and denting, as well as erosion from most types of chemicals. There are a number of different colors available, making cast iron tubs the top choice for many homeowners. On the downside, these tubs are extremely heavy and may require extra labor to install.

PORCELAIN ENAMEL ON STEEL

Also sometimes called pressed steel, this is another inexpensive and very common bathtub material. The tub is stamped from a thin sheet of steel then finished with a layer of porcelain enamel. These tubs are durable and easy to clean. The finish is resistant to most common chemicals, and it retains its gloss for a long time. They're also convenient when replacing fiberglass or acrylic tub/shower units, as they fit in the same 5-foot opening and can be finished off nicely with a ceramic tile surround. On the downside, they're heavier than fiberglass and acrylic, the surface can rust and chip under impact, and the number of shapes and sizes available is very limited.

REMODELING OPTIONS FOR THE BATHTUB AND SHOWER BASE

As with most fixtures in the bathroom, there are multiple options available depending on what you're starting with. Because this book is about small, standard-sized bathrooms, we will assume that you're either dealing with a standard 5' bathtub (either porcelain or fiberglass) or a fiberglass or acrylic shower base. You will also most likely either have a one-piece or three-piece shower enclosure. A three-piece shower enclosure can be easily disassembled and taken out of the room if you want to replace it. However, a one-piece shower enclosure must be cut down into smaller pieces as they are typically installed before the door jambs and drywall and will not fit through the bathroom door. If you have a bathtub or shower base (meaning a three-piece enclosure), regardless of what material it's made of, you also have some type of shower walls installed above the tub or shower base. Those are typically tiled walls or some variation of a three-piece shower wall system installed above the tub or shower base.

Bathtubs and shower bases are a good case for the "good," "better," and "best" scenarios. Let's start by looking at all of the options and asking a couple of questions. First of all, what's the condition of the existing bathtub or shower? Is the fixture structurally sound (meaning though it may be ugly or dated, it still functions properly)? Let's look at all the possible scenarios.

1. Use the existing tub or shower base.

   a. Keep the current bathtub or shower base as is. This assumes it's structurally sound and cosmetically acceptable, maybe needing only minor cleaning or caulking.

b. Keep the current bathtub or shower base, but have it refinished or relined if possible.

2. Replace the bathtub or shower base.

   a. Have a new bathtub or shower base installed, which will require new shower wet walls to also be replaced. More on this in Chapter 3.

BATHTUB AND SHOWER BASE OPTIONS (GOOD, BETTER, BEST SCENARIOS)

The "GOOD" Option

This option is available when the fixture is in good enough condition that you can consider reusing it.

This option is great because it really doesn't cost you much. Oftentimes, a bathroom needing remodeling can be achieved without doing much to the shower area. In fact, sometimes, just a thorough cleaning can be enough. Some professional grout cleaning or basic removal and replacement of caulking can make all the difference. Sometimes, adding a shower door or replacing an old one can also have a significant impact in making an older shower look new again.

Additionally, don't forget accessories. Using upgraded towel bars and new colorful towels alone can change the feeling of the room.

The "BETTER" Option

When reusing the existing fixture is possible but cleaning or caulking just isn't enough, consider bathtub refinishing or relining.

Short of replacement—which is option three—restoring your existing fixture can be a fantastic option instead of ripping out and replacing or doing nothing. Restoration is a huge secret in bathroom remodeling.

Bathtub Refinishing

Refinishing your bathtub or shower base saves hundreds or even thousands of dollars over replacement. Refinishing a tub will take hours instead of days. While the price of a brand-new bathtub or shower base may seem affordable at first, there are many other costs associated with a bathtub or shower base replacement. Replacement requires removal and disposal of the old bathtub or shower fixture, plumbing, flooring, and shower wet wall work. According to Home Advisor, the national average to replace a bathtub is between $4,122 and $10,737, including labor and materials, while bathtub refinishing can start as low as a few hundred dollars.[6] The durability of a refinished bathtub or shower base is much the same as a brand-new one, so if the structure itself can be saved, you could save thousands.

Refinishing is a spraying process with an industrial coating made exclusively for the bathtub, ceramic tile, and countertop refinishing industry. The fixture is cleaned, sanded, and repaired where needed. Then, it is typically primed with a two-component (two-part) epoxy-based primer, followed by a top coat or finishing coat (white or clear). The top coat is usually an aliphatic acrylic polyurethane that will hold its gloss retention for years and has UV properties, eliminating fading and yellowing. Refinishing coatings have been on the market for decades now, are extremely chemical resistant, and will create and maintain a shine like the original surface.

Bathtub refinishing should be professionally applied because it is based on sound chemistry and meticulous preparation. The failure or success of every job is determined by the skill of the technician doing the refinishing and the quality of the products they use. Having realistic expectations of what a successful job is has a lot to do with your overall happiness of the finished job. I always tell my clients that if they expect perfection, they'll be left disappointed. Refinishing is a restoration project, not a brand-new product.

When you decide to refinish a bathtub or shower base (or anything, for that matter), you are choosing to have a new coating hand-laid over the existing finish. The fixture will never look 100% new again but should look very close to new. It is normal to see small imperfections in the finish, like how it may not feel totally smooth upon completion, having a slight 'orange peel' texture. These are normal results upon the completion of a refinishing job. However, with use, many of the small imperfections will typically wear down and become less noticeable over time. There's really nothing that can't be refinished; however, rusted fixtures are not recommended to refinish, as rust typically returns and may shorten the lifespan of the refinished surface. However, it may still make sense depending on your budget and how long you need the remodel to last.

FIGURE 2.1

BEFORE

AFTER

What a difference a couple of hours make! This tub and tile surround was refinished in bright white after removing the old shower door and repairing the holes. Notice that the countertop was not replaced nor was the room's paint color changed, but it made a huge difference just refinishing the tub and tile without ripping anything out. The total cost came to $1,200 and took just a day and a half to complete.

Bathtub Liner

If you have a porcelain tub, you may have another option: a bathtub liner. The bathtub liner is another great alternative to replacement but only works on porcelain bathtubs. Plastic bathtub and shower bases are not candidates for this type of service. To install a liner, a professional company comes to your home and measures and photographs the porcelain tub. The photos are then sent to a manufacturer that creates a new shell, which is roughly a quarter-inch thick, molded acrylic insert to place over the old tub. After receiving the manufactured shell, the company will deliver and install it on top of the existing tub, a process that only takes a day.

A bathtub liner is more expensive than refinishing, costing roughly $1,100 to $1,400 (or more if you install a wall unit). However, a bathtub liner is still typically cheaper than replacing a tub, and it offers several advantages. One benefit of liners is that you can also order a matching shower wall system with built-in shelves and storage areas which are designed to install directly over the existing tile walls. So, if your tile walls are also in rough shape, a full liner system that covers both the tub and the wet walls can instantly improve the look of your bathroom without a messy tear out.

FIGURE 2.2

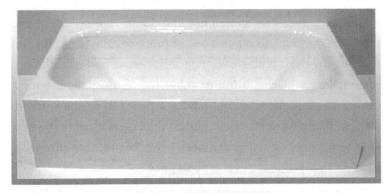

UNINSTALLED BATHTUB LINER

INSTALLED BATHTUB LINER

This quarter-inch bathtub shell was trimmed to fit directly on top of an old porcelain bathtub. The drain and overflow holes were cut for the new drain and overflow plate during installation. The tub liner was set directly on top of the old tub and adhered with rubber butyl tape in between the two tubs. The entire tub liner was sealed with a white silicone sealant to the existing tile walls and tile floor. The total installation time was 3-4 hours, and the tub was ready to use the following day.

The "BEST" Option

As stated earlier, sometimes the "best" option is not the preferred option. This may be one of those situations. In addition to being the most time-consuming and invasive part of bathroom remodeling, replacing a tub or shower is also usually the most expensive step. It's true that having a new tub or shower with all new plumbing underneath and behind it will provide the best long-term option, but if you're looking to take the more affordable road on your project, this is probably not it.

One of the reasons that replacing the bathtub and shower is so costly and intrusive is that it's the foundation of the room. Everything is built on top of the tub or shower base, and so many other fixtures are affected when you remove them, including the bathroom floor, plumbing drain, water supply plumbing valve, shower walls, shower door, and the demolition of drywall. All of the trades that need to be involved when installing a new tub or shower base will very quickly add time and cost to the remodel.

Here is what you can expect from the costs associated with all of the options. If you can clean up and caulk your existing tub or shower, it will cost you typically less than $100. If you refinish your tub or shower, it will cost you roughly less than $1,000. If you go the bathtub liner route (when applicable), it will cost you between $1,000 and $2,000. Finally, the full replacement will cost you well over $2,000 depending on the new tub or shower.

My suggestion is to get some help deciding on the best course of action for your tub/shower. Get some professional opinions and quotes on your project, including contractors from different fields such as traditional remodeling and bathtub refinishing. Your decision will be more informative with some solid professional advice.

CHAPTER
THREE

BATHTUB/SHOWER
WET WALLS

How you remodel your shower walls will have a major impact on your entire bathroom. Just like bathtubs, shower walls are made of many types of materials. Also like bathtubs, replacing shower walls is an expensive and complex task that can take days and get messy.

Most homes, especially tract homes, have one of two types of bathtubs installed in them. As we learned in Chapter 1, you more than likely have either a porcelain tub or a fiberglass one-piece tub/shower combo. The type of tub you install dictates the type of shower walls you have.

FIBERGLASS BATHTUB/SHOWER COMBO

A one-piece fiberglass and acrylic shower unit or stall is one of the most efficient, budget-friendly choices when you are building a home, which is why so many builders use them. For the sake of this chapter, we will refer to all of the plastic types of bathtubs as fiberglass enclosures since they are the most common. These one-piece tub/shower combos are built in factories using molds, and they show up on a construction site ready to install, unlike porcelain bathtubs which require wet walls installed above them. If you have a fiberglass bathtub or shower in the room that you are remodeling, you really only have two choices.

Refinishing a Fiberglass Bathtub Enclosure

The "good" option—and maybe the only reasonable option when you have a fiberglass enclosure—is to refinish it, assuming that cleaning it is not enough to make it look good again. Since it's a one-piece unit, the shower walls and tub are one solid unit, so there's no changing just one part. Since bathtub liners only reline the tub portion of a porcelain tub, they are not an option with fiberglass or acrylic enclosures, leaving refinishing as the only non-replacement option. The good news is that this is a great option, as not only is refinishing fiberglass and acrylic tubs affordable compared to other remodeling options, but also because the plastic-based tubs are softer than porcelain, refinish well, are durable, and hold up for a long time if they're properly maintained.

FIGURE 3.1

BEFORE

AFTER

In this remodel, the existing fiberglass tub/shower enclosure was completely refinished, and the old tub plumbing trim was replaced.

Notice that the old shower door was removed and the holes left from the door were repaired prior to refinishing. The old toilet was replaced with a new, elongated design that replaced the dated, round design. The entire room was repainted, and a colorful shower curtain was installed. The bathroom door was also replaced with a raised six-panel door with new hinges, a door knob, and a coat of paint. We finished off this smart remodel for less than $2,000.

Replacing a Fiberglass Bathtub Enclosure

The "best" option when there's a fiberglass enclosure would be a complete tear out. As you can probably guess, this is almost never recommended if you're on a budget unless you're looking to really change the entire look of the room and have the dollars to do so.

There is nothing that can't be repaired on a damaged fiberglass bathtub. This includes cracks, holes, soft tub floors, and even holes cut in the wall by a plumber to repair plumbing valves. All of these situations can be professionally and properly repaired and refinished. With that said, if you still decide to remove the enclosure, there are a few things to be aware of when removing the old unit.

Most fiberglass tub enclosures are larger than the bathroom door opening. That means they were installed during the framing process when the room was new, and you will not be able to fit another one into the small room. The old unit will need to be cut and hauled out of the bathroom in pieces. Once the old unit is out of the bathroom, a standalone tub will need to be installed with new shower wet walls as a one-piece unit is no longer an option. If another fiberglass or acrylic unit is desired, many products come with a tub and three-piece interlocking wall units that are reasonably priced and can be installed by any professional or qualified handyman. This option consists of a set of components that fit together to create a smooth, watertight surface for your shower's interior. The set usually includes a shower pan or bathtub, plus one or more pieces for the walls.

A standalone wall kit can also be used. A prefab shower wall kit includes the wall pieces by themselves without the shower pan or bathtub. This can be a good option as it allows you to choose the bathtub or shower pan that you want, and the wall kit installs directly above the tub or shower.

TILE SHOWER WALLS

If you do not have a fiberglass enclosure, then you almost certainly have a porcelain bathtub or some sort of composite shower pan that has tile shower walls installed above it. As you can probably guess at this point, there are several options to choose from when trying to do an affordable remodel. Let's separate these options into two categories: restoration and replacement.

Restoring the Existing Tile Shower Walls

Restoring or replacing tile shower walls really comes down to personal preferences and budget. If you like your existing tile or stone, and if it's in good enough condition to keep it, then you're saving yourself a big chunk of money by not having to do anything. Moreover, if you like the walls but they have some issues, such as tile or grout deterioration or water damage, then there are a few things you can do to save them. Like with restoring a porcelain bathtub as outlined in Chapter 2, you can do a lot with tile shower walls just by cleaning them really well and having some recaulking done. This may be enough to make the tile look new again and will save more money than the next options.

Another option, assuming you can live with the tile walls and the tiles are structurally sound, is regrouting. There are professional companies that will come in and remove the top layer of the existing grout, regrout the entire shower, and reseal all the new grout. This is a fairly affordable option. One benefit is that you have the option of being able to change the grout color, which could bring a whole new look to an older shower.

Let's assume that replacing the tile walls is not in your budget, but the existing tile is either an undesirable color, cracked, damaged, or worn past the point of being able to be cleaned. In this case, a professional refinishing company can repair and refinish the entire tile shower wall for a fraction of the cost of replacement. The benefits of refinishing old tile are many, including not only the ability to change the color of the tile, but also the endless options to refinish the tile in multi-color schemes, simulating solid surface products like Corian and even natural stone. Furthermore, when tile is refinished, the grout must also be included, so the grout gets repaired and sealed all in the same job.

FIGURE 3.2

BEFORE

AFTER

This small 45 sq. ft. bathroom had a major makeover on a shoestring budget. The bathtub and tile shower walls were refinished in white (hiding the pink!), and new shower trim was installed. The old, single-pane bathroom window was replaced with a double-pane, white vinyl retrofit window. The old vanity cabinet and tile countertop were replaced with an affordable vanity pack that included the cabinet, granite top, and recessed sink. Just the faucet was added. The toilet was replaced as well as the flooring. Notice that the old 1960s wallpaper was removed, the walls were textured to match the rest of the bathroom, and the entire room was painted. The framed vanity mirror and light fixture were both purchased at garage sales for a total of $35.

Replacing Tile Shower Walls

If you have the budget and want to give your imagination free reign to create a unique shower that's perfectly suited to the style of your new look, then ceramic, porcelain, or natural stone tiles are your best options. These tiles come in a nearly endless array of sizes, colors, and textures and can be mixed and matched for a one-of-a-kind design. If the idea of customizing your shower walls doesn't appeal to you, though, you can keep things simple by tiling your shower with a single, neutral color. Although new tile walls cost more than restoring old tile, installing new tile will potentially give your remodel a more modern or upscale look and may be worth the extra money.

One secret trick that I have exercised many times—especially when buying and flipping homes—is installing new tile over existing tile. This can't always be done, but in most cases, assuming the existing walls are structurally sound, new ceramic tile or stone can be installed directly on top of the old wet wall. This method is great because there is no messy demolition required and you can customize the shower without a costly tear out. While doing this in the past, I have taken the new tile or stone all the way up to the ceiling, extending the walls and dramatically changing the look of the shower.

Many tile setters may not be familiar with installing new tile or stone over the existing tile. They may not be comfortable with this and will recommend tearing out the old tile instead. My suggestion is to have it quoted both ways and factor in not only the added expenses of the demolition and wall prep, but also the mess, extra time involved, and risk of damaging the existing tub or shower pan.

If your project will require you to replace the tile walls, then regardless of which installation method you choose, you will need to decide on a type of tile or stone. Although ceramic and porcelain are essentially the same material, they have slightly different properties. Porcelain is denser, more water-resistant, and more durable than ceramic. On the other hand, ceramic is traditionally less expensive and easier to work with than porcelain. The installation cost of either should be the same, and I've found that you can find very affordable selections of both if you shop around, so for me, the decision comes down to design.

Ceramic and porcelain tiles typically cost less than stone, as natural stone is considered higher end, although prices for higher-end tiles can sometimes even surpass those of cheaper stone tiles. Because natural stone is more porous than ceramic or porcelain tiles, it more readily absorbs water, soap, minerals in the water, and grime. The tiles are sealed to prevent this but the sealant wears off, so you'll need to reseal your stone tiles regularly according to the sealant manufacturer's recommendations. The choices of natural stone include marble, granite, travertine, or slate, and each material has its pros and cons. Marble looks opulent but is prone to staining and absorbing water. Travertine is richly colored, easy to cut, and can be a great value, but it is susceptible to scratching and staining.[7] Slate is durable, but it's a challenge to install evenly due to its naturally layered structure.

Natural stone will normally be the most expensive choice for shower walls, but it's not necessarily as durable as ceramic and porcelain tiles. If replacing your old tile walls is what you decide to do, you have many good options to upgrade this space at an affordable price.

CHAPTER FOUR

CABINETS

Other than the tub and shower walls, cabinets can be the second most expensive item or fixture in a bathroom remodel. Well-made cabinets aren't cheap, especially if you have a nonstandard size. Bathroom cabinets located beneath the sink can be expensive compared to other remodeling fixtures like faucets, sinks, toilets, and even flooring. Cabinets can take a big chunk out of your remodeling budget.

Cabinets are another case for the "good," "better," and "best" scenarios. Let's start by looking at all of the options and asking a couple of questions. First of all, do you have what's considered a standard industry-sized cabinet? What's the condition of the existing cabinet? Is it structurally sound? Let's look at all the possible scenarios.

USE THE EXISTING CABINET OR REPLACE WITH A NEW ONE? CABINET REMODELING OPTIONS

Use the Existing Cabinet

- Keep the current cabinet as is. This assumes it's structurally sound and cosmetically acceptable.
- Keep the current cabinet and only paint or refinish it. Maybe the cabinet is in good shape, but you want a different looking exterior.

Replace the Cabinet

- Purchase a prefabricated, standard-sized cabinet in a box, no assembly required.
- Purchase a standard-sized cabinet that you will need to assemble.
- Have a cabinet maker custom build a cabinet for you.

CABINET OPTIONS (GOOD, BETTER, BEST SCENARIOS)

The "GOOD" Option

The good option is available when the cabinet is in a good enough condition to consider reusing it.

Doing nothing except cleaning your existing cabinet is the least expensive option, only takes a little time, and is without a doubt the easiest option. If your existing cabinet is in reasonably good shape, functions well, and you like it enough to live with it, then you have just saved yourself a fair amount of cost and effort.

The other "good" option, which is the next least expensive way to remodel your bathroom as far as your cabinets are concerned, is to clean, sand, and either paint or restain the existing cabinet. This is a great option when you have a really limited budget or when you are trying to put more money into another fixture and only have so many dollars to work with.

Maybe you need to replace the tub because it's rusted, or maybe the tiles are falling off the walls and can't be refinished or saved. Sometimes you don't have a choice, so you save and reuse the fixtures that you can. Oftentimes, cabinets can be saved by simply giving them a new look.

Refinishing your cabinet is a great low-cost option and can typically be done by a homeowner. The look you want is only limited by your imagination. You can do so many different finishes, such as fauxing, crackling, or some sort of specialty finish, which is a fun do-it-yourself project. You can also just sand and paint the cabinet in a solid color that is brushed, rolled, or sprayed. Then, of course, it can be sanded and restained if it's already a solid wood cabinet.

If you do choose to keep the cabinet, changing the hinges and knobs is typically easy. For less than $100, you can makeover an existing cabinet to look beautiful and stand alongside the rest of the fixtures in the bathroom.

One word of caution: if you do decide to use your existing cabinet, be sure it's what you really want. Once you start installing countertops, sinks, and plumbing around the cabinet, it gets expensive to change your mind. Make sure you're happy with the inside of the cabinet, the drawers properly function, and you can replace the hinges with the same size. Sometimes, trying to save a penny can cost you a dime down the road if you aren't careful.

FIGURE 4.1

BEFORE

AFTER

A nicely remodeled guest bathroom using the existing cabinet, countertop, tub, and tile wet walls. The large cabinet was faux painted to look like wood, and new knobs were added, saving time and money. The aging full-length mirror was changed out for a modern-looking dual-mirror set, and the existing undermount sinks were replaced with new top-mounted sinks and faucets. The large vanity countertop would have been very expensive to replace but instead was refinished with a multi-colored granite finish. Notice that the floor was tiled with 16 x 16 travertine, which replaced the old bathroom carpet. The tub and tile walls were in good structural condition and were cleaned and recaulked. The toilet was also replaced, and the entire room was repainted. The total cost for this 11 x 5 bathroom was under $3,000 and took less than a week to complete.

The "BETTER" Option

When reusing the existing cabinet is not an option, prefabricated assembled bath cabinets are a great option.

The next step up from using your existing cabinet is replacing it. The least expensive way to purchase a new cabinet is to buy a cabinet that is prefabricated, or prebuilt and ready to be installed. This can be done in several ways.

Most people will find that the big-box stores will have a variety of cabinets that will suit them somewhere between 24 and 48 inches long or even 60 inches, but in most standard 5 x 9 square foot bathrooms, it's probably going to be a 36" to a 42" or a 48" cabinet. Prefabricated cabinets are not considered a top-quality choice when compared to custom-made cabinets, but once you get them installed, get the countertop on them, and get everything screwed in and caulked, they work well (see Figure 4.2).

The upgraded option to a prefabricated cabinet, which is what I've done many times over the years, is going to a shop that sells quality unassembled boxed cabinets. These shops are typically found in larger cities and may be kitchen and bath stores that stock granite slabs and cabinets. Many times, they are an import business that brings in products from overseas. Shops like these are great resources as they usually sell cabinets that are boxed and will need to be assembled but are in stock for immediate pickup. The cabinets I have used the most are manufactured in China. There are many styles and sizes to choose from, and they are a great, low-cost option as long as you have a standard size.

These cabinets can usually be built in roughly 30 minutes per cabinet. So, let's say you have a 60-inch cabinet. You probably won't find a 60-inch cabinet all in one piece. You might use two 30-inch cabinets and connect them together. Most standard size bathrooms likely only have one sink, so you would only need one cabinet. However, if you did have two or more cabinets, you would individually purchase them and install them together as one.

The thing about doing it this way, whether you're building them yourself or hiring a good handyman to put them together, is that once they're assembled, they look like custom cabinets.

They will need a toe kick (a piece of wood that goes along the bottom of the cabinet) to match, and you typically need scribe molding on the side, which is a finished trim piece that covers up the gap between the cabinet and the wall. Walls are never perfectly level, and cabinets usually don't sit perfectly flush to the wall.

As you can see, there are extra steps down this route, but if you're having a contractor redo a bathroom and you're trying to keep the costs down, this is the best way to build a nice cabinet and not have it cost a fortune, as these cabinets can be affordable. You have to do a little bit of legwork, and you have to do the assembly and installation, but you'll end up with a great product.

Most of these import cabinets are excellent quality. Many have higher-quality plywood backs, sides, and shelving rather than pressed wood, the doors usually have soft-close hinges, and the drawers are tongue and groove construction.

FIGURE 4.2

BEFORE

AFTER

This small 45 sq. ft. bathroom was remodeled in just three days for roughly $2,500. The vanity cabinet and countertop were purchased pre-assembled from The Home Depot, and a new faucet was installed. The *mirror and vanity light were replaced. The shower valve was updated as well as the angle stop valves and supply lines. The bathtub was repaired and refinished, and the entire bathroom was painted. New towel bars and wall accessories were installed. Both the flooring and elongated toilet were cleaned and reused.*

Know Where Your Plumbing Is Located

Plumbing will most likely be the part of your bathroom that dictates where your vanity is going to go. It costs time and money to make changes to plumbing, and assuming you're replacing the cabinet with the same size and design, you shouldn't have any issues. Many homeowners and remodelers get themselves in trouble with plumbing location when a cabinet design gets modified from the original. For example, adding a drawer bank may encroach on existing plumbing inside the cabinet space and require the plumbing to be modified. Moving plumbing is not impossible but will add time and expense to the project. A good rule of thumb when doing an affordable remodel is to try to use the existing plumbing locations.

The "BEST" Option

If you have a larger budget and want something specific from a prefabricated or semi-custom line, or if you have a unique size situation, then having a cabinet built specifically for your project may be the way to go. This option gives nearly infinite options, because anything is available if you have someone make it—any size, any finish, any door style, and any other type of custom feature. However, in most remodels—and in this book, we are focusing on the affordable side of remodels—a custom cabinet typically isn't in the cards for most people, nor does it have to be.

TIMEFRAMES FOR CABINETS

Ordering custom-made cabinets from a local cabinet maker could take anywhere from two to eight weeks. Ordering from a national builder (semi-custom) usually takes around four to eight weeks. Semi-custom cabinets are a good option if you have time, but be warned that they often get damaged in shipping, which can cause delays in your project.

If you live near a major city where you can find prefabricated or boxed import cabinets, you'll be able to speed up your project and probably be able to have the cabinet on the same day, assuming it's in stock.

CHAPTER
FIVE

VANITY TOPS

Bathroom countertops, or vanity tops, are a very important part of your bathroom remodel. The countertop in the bathroom not only provides a functional work surface but is also where people stand to get ready for their day. It's where they place their toiletries and other personal items, and it's typically the first thing we see when we enter the room. A good bathroom countertop is the right blend of aesthetic and durability that's sufficient to meet the demands of how you live. It's a big part of the decorating as well.

One thing that needs to be mentioned here is that your vanity top may or may not include an integrated sink bowl. Many builders used cultured marble (manufactured marble) tops when building the home because of their durability, low cost, and ease of installation. Some of these cultured marble sinks are molded into the countertop as one-piece units, whereas others were installed with a bottom mount or top mount (self-rimming) sink cut into them. It's important to recognize the difference and know not only what you currently have but also what you want should you choose to replace the existing countertop during the remodel.

You have some options when it comes to upgrading your vanity top. In terms of what's "good," "better," or "best," you will have to choose whether you can use the existing top or replace it with a new one. Here are the options for vanity top improvements:

USING THE EXISTING VANITY TOP

Keep the current countertop as is. This assumes it's structurally sound and cosmetically acceptable with just minor cleaning and recaulking. This option costs little to nothing.

Keep the current cabinet and have it refinished.

REPLACING THE VANITY TOP

Purchase a prefabricated, standard-sized countertop, which typically includes the sink.

Have a fabricator custom build a countertop for you.

VANITY TOP OPTIONS (GOOD, BETTER, AND BEST SCENARIOS)

The "GOOD" Option

The "good" option is available when the countertop is in good enough condition to consider reusing it.

Like with any other fixture in your project room, doing nothing except cleaning and recaulking your existing counter is the least expensive option, only taking a little time. Without a doubt, it's the easiest way to go. However, if you are replacing your bathroom cabinet, I would not recommend trying to cut costs by reinstalling your old countertop, as new vanity tops often come included with a cabinet or, if purchased separately, are typically not a larger cost of your overall remodel budget. With that said—and depending on how tight your budget is—if your existing counter is in reasonably good shape, functions well, and you like it enough to live with it, then once again, you have just saved yourself a fair amount of money and effort.

But since you're looking to improve the room, you may decide that you want to make a change with the countertop. The other "good" option, which is the next least expensive way to remodel your bathroom as far as your countertop is concerned, is to have it refinished. This is a great option when you are using the existing cabinet, have a really limited budget, or are trying to put more money into another fixture and only have so many dollars to work with. Refinishing the vanity top is a great, low-cost option, can typically be done by a professional in one day, and will allow you a host of options to choose from to completely transform your countertop. On projects I've completed in the past, I've chosen to have the vanity top refinished in a granite, multicolored look to match the tile shower walls, providing a great design tie-in.

FIGURE 5.1

BEFORE

AFTER

This vanity area was remodeled using the existing cabinet (just adding knobs), the existing mirror, and the existing sink. We refinished over the existing vanity countertop with a multi-colored granite finish. Notice that the sink faucet was replaced as well as the medicine cabinet. Also, notice how the door jamb casing was upgraded while the entire space was repainted.

The "BETTER" Option

The "better" alternative is available when reusing the existing vanity top is not an option.

As said previously, if you're replacing the cabinet, then you'll definitely want to replace the vanity top, too. Regardless, if you need to replace the vanity top, it is a relatively easy and not very costly part of the remodeling process.

Just like standard-sized cabinets, vanity tops also come in standard sizes to accommodate them. Most big-box home improvement stores have a variety of vanity tops that fit on top of standard-sized cabinets, ranging from 24" to 60".

The "BEST" Option

If you have a larger budget and want something specific that you can't find in a premade size, you may need to have a fabricator measure and fabricate the countertop for you. As in custom cabinetry, this option will give you the most choices because anything is available if you have someone make it—any size, any material, a custom backsplash, and so on. However, this option should really be your last option, as selecting affordable fixtures is essential to keeping the overall remodel within your budget.

If you're purchasing a cabinet from an import remodeling shop that also sells prefabricated granite slabs, you may consider having your contractor or handyman also install a higher-end vanity top, which would be a nice upgrade that may not break the bank. I have used this option on many of my remodels, and I've been able to upgrade a bathroom with a granite top for about the same cost as a lower-quality, prefabricated, cultured marble vanity top. When going this route, you will need to purchase a sink to install into the granite, so while there is a little more involvement in the installation process, it may be worth looking into.

FIGURE 5.2

BEFORE

AFTER

This small 9 x 5 ft bathroom was remodeled in just four days for roughly $4,000. The existing floors and wall tiles were removed along with the vanity cabinet and counter. The vanity cabinet was purchased out of a box, assembled, and installed. A prefabricated granite countertop was *purchased and installed with a top mount sink bowl and new faucet. The mirror and vanity light were replaced as well as a new elongated toilet. The shower trim was replaced after the one-piece fiberglass enclosure was refinished, and new shower doors were installed. 16 x 16 ceramic tiles were installed on the floor, and the bathroom was painted.*

CHAPTER
SIX

BATHROOM
SINKS

Sinks go hand in hand with vanity tops. As discussed in the previous chapter, many sinks come included with a vanity top, either mounted to the top or underside of the counter or molded in as an integral sink bowl. This chapter assumes that you are either using or restoring your existing countertop with a removable sink, or you are replacing the vanity top and need to install a sink.

Another thing to note is how many sinks are currently in your bathroom. Oftentimes, when remodeling a bathroom, we believe that adding a sink will increase the value of the room. Sometimes this is true, and it may add to the feeling of luxury that we're trying to achieve.

However, when remodeling a small bathroom, more isn't always better. While two sinks help ease morning traffic, especially for large families, they also reduce countertop space. You may need to ask yourself if double sinks with little countertop space are more useful than a single sink with more surface space.

Additionally, adding a second sink is expensive. It adds cost with the expense of the extra sink, as well as the faucet, but the priciest part is the increase in plumbing costs, as it requires the addition of hot and cold supply lines as well as a waste line. This plumbing would all need to be done inside the wall. When I remodel small bathrooms, I try to keep the original size and layout of the existing room.

Replacing a sink is not an expensive part of the total cost of the remodel. If you're using your existing vanity top, your choices are determined by the hole already cut in the counter, and you are probably left with replacing the old sink.

The next chapter covers plumbing fixtures; they tie into the sink, as most sinks hold the bathroom faucet. When you're replacing the sink, it's a good time to install the faucet before it gets mounted into the vanity top.

DETERMINE YOUR SINK STYLE

While sink choices are limited when using your existing vanity top, they're endless when you're replacing a countertop that doesn't have a hole for the sink yet. Though price is always a consideration, you'll also need to think about the bowl's shape, design, and how it will impact the look and utility of your counter.

With so many sink styles available, it can be a little overwhelming trying to pick your favorite. The best way to approach it is to decide how much counter space you want and how much should be allotted to the sink. A sink will take up some of the countertop no matter the style, but depending on which one you go with, you can minimize the amount of counter space it requires. Compare standard sinks with vessel, undermount, and all-in-one styles to get a better idea of how you want your own vanity set up.

FIGURE 6.1

This is an example of an interestingly shaped vessel sink installed in a granite vanity top. Notice the added height of the plumbing faucet and that it's a single-handle fixture drilled into the granite.

The size of your sink will also depend on your priorities for the countertop. If you're working with a limited surface area, a smaller sink will help you make the most of your space and make the room feel larger.

CHAPTER
SEVEN

PLUMBING
FIXTURES

To start the discussion of bathroom plumbing, we should take a look at all of the plumbing required to make a bathroom operational. Some of the plumbing in the bathroom is in plain sight and very noticeable, like the sink faucet or the shower drain. However, much of the plumbing that is necessary for your bathroom to operate properly is not easily seen and is either inside a cabinet or built into the walls. Understanding plumbing parts is important when doing a remodel and can save you time, money, and unnecessary headaches. Keeping with the theme of this book, this chapter will address the identification of all the plumbing in the bathroom and include some tips on what should be replaced and what you could (and should) leave alone.

The main plumbing components in every bathroom are:
- The bathtub/shower faucet
- The sink faucet
- Faucet shut-off valves and supply lines
- Waste drains
- Toilets (We will leave toilets out of this chapter, as it is covered in depth in Chapter 11.)

BATHTUB/SHOWER FAUCET

We start with the bathtub/shower faucet because it can be the toughest, most expensive plumbing part in your remodel. In the industry, we call the tub/shower faucet the shower valve or mixing valve, which is how we will refer to it moving forward. The shower valve has two parts to it: the actual valve, which is behind the shower wall, and the trim that attaches to the valve, which is the part that we see and appreciate.

The Shower Valve

The valve is exactly that—a mechanical valve that connects to the hot and cold pipes in the wall and regulates the water temperature for the shower. Your house's age could determine what type of shower valve you have. In older homes, especially those built before 1960, there will likely be a traditional mixing valve with two or three separate handles, two if it's only a shower and three if it's a tub/shower. This type of valve does not regulate or balance the hot water coming into the shower and will not regulate sudden changes in water pressure, so someone showering runs a risk of getting scalded if a sink, toilet, or washing machine unexpectedly draws out cold water.

Single-handle valves may or may not be pressure-regulated. Building codes now require safer shower valves, so it's important to know what you currently have. A local plumber will be able to educate you on what you have and let you know what's available for your application should you be replacing it.

Pressure-balancing valves, or anti-scald valves, are the most common type of shower valve. A pressure-balancing valve is designed to rebalance water pressure to keep the shower from becoming excessively hot or cold. If you've ever showered in a pre-1980s home, you know that if someone turns on the hot water in another part of the house, your shower water will turn ice cold. Pressure-balancing valves counteract this. The mechanisms contain pistons or diaphragms built to move with fluctuations in water pressure to balance the hot and cold water supplies. These can keep the water temperature constant within two to three degrees Fahrenheit.

FIGURE 7.1

This is an example of a Moen pressure-balanced shower valve. This is the portion of the plumbing that's inside the wall. Notice the small shutoff screws that allow the water to be shut off here at the valve with a flathead screwdriver rather than shutting the water off for the entire property. This is helpful when a plumber needs to service the valve or change the cartridge.

If you've read this far, the question you probably have is whether or not you need to change your shower valve. The answer: maybe. It depends on what your plans are with your existing shower walls.

If you have already identified your valve to be a pressure-balanced valve, then it is probably unnecessary to replace your existing valve. If you don't have a pressure-balanced valve, but you have a fiberglass enclosure or tile walls, it may be difficult to replace the valve unless a plumber can access the valve through the drywall or exterior wall on the back side. If you're refinishing a fiberglass enclosure or tile walls, then you could have a plumber cut a hole in the fiberglass or remove some tiles, and the refinishing company could repair the hole made by the plumber prior to refinishing.

If you've decided (or if you have to) remove your existing shower walls and you do not currently have a pressure-balanced valve, then I would recommend you replace it.

FIGURE 7.2

BEFORE

DURING

AFTER

In this remodel, the old three-handle, non-pressure-balanced shower valve was replaced with a new, modern pressure-balancing single-handle design. Though the plumber had access from a closet behind the tub to install the new shower valve, there were still several unwanted holes that had to be repaired during the refinishing prep process. After installing the new shower valve, the unwanted holes were repaired, and the entire enclosure was refinished in bright white. The fixture not only looked new again, but the old 1970s plumbing was also upgraded and looks amazing!

The Shower Trim

The shower trim (or shower faucet) is the part of the shower plumbing that we can see. It's the shiny chrome, stainless, gold, or bronze-finished handles, tub spout, and showerhead that you may want to replace. Replacing the shower valve trim is a great way to inexpensively upgrade your existing shower without having to go behind the wall. Replacing the faucets for your tub and shower can be easy and inexpensive if you go about it the right way. Regardless of whether your current valve is pressure-balanced or not, as long as it works properly, you should be able to replace only your shower trim. In order to determine if a trim kit is available for your particular tub and shower faucet, you will first need to determine the brand and style of the valve you have. Again, a local plumber, hardware shop, or big-box store may help match it up if you remove the trim and bring it to them.

I'll share a secret tip here that I have used several times during my career. Oftentimes, the shower valve is operational and the shower trim is in good shape, but it's the wrong finish or looks aged. Plus, because it's old, replacement trim is no longer available. As a fix, I have successfully removed the shower trim and prepped and painted the handles and escutcheon plate, the circular metal disk that hides the pipes, to match some of the newer plumbing trim in the room. This works well when the rest of the new trim is oil-rubbed bronze. I have been able to find spray cans locally that matched close enough to make the painted parts look like they had been replaced.

VANITY FAUCETS

The vanity faucet is one thing that I usually replace, no matter what type of bathroom remodel I'm doing. The faucet is an affordable piece of the remodel that, no matter what the remodeling plan is for the vanity and sink, will improve the look of the bathroom for very little cost and effort. However, faucets are not a "one size fits all" and not all faucets work with every sink, so it's important to make sure the faucet you choose fits your sink or countertop.

Let's take a look at the three different types of vanity faucets. They are centerset, single-hole, and widespread. What makes them fundamentally different from each other is how they're installed into the sink or countertop. There are a different number of holes required to install them properly.

Four-Inch Centerset

Four-inch centerset faucets are made for sinks with three holes and have handles that are four inches apart. They combine handles and a spout on a single base unit. Some centerset faucets may have two handles mounted onto a six-inch plate. The four-inch centerset faucet is the most common of all faucets and typically the least expensive while offering the largest selection of choices.

Single-Hole

A single-hole bathroom faucet most commonly has only one handle. If your sink has only one hole drilled in it, then this is your only option. However, sinks with a four-inch centerset drill can accommodate a single-hole faucet by using the included optional plate which will cover up the extra holes.

Vessel sinks, bowl or basin-shaped sinks that sit on top of counters, have become more common in recent years and can look good if you've decided to replace your vanity top. The faucet needed for a vessel bowl is typically a single-hole design but taller. The vessel faucet needs to sit higher than a traditional sink and usually comes with a single, multifunction handle.

Widespread

Widespread bathroom faucets work with wider drilled three-hole sinks or countertops that have been drilled larger than four inches. The faucet consists of three separate pieces—two handles and a spout—and the spacing between the handles ranges from six to sixteen inches. However, the spacing is typically eight inches. I like the eight-inch widespread faucet the most out of all the faucet types because I think it looks the most elegant and is easy to clean. However, there are typically fewer of this size to choose from, and they tend to be more expensive than the four-inch centerset or single-hole variety. The eight-inch widespread faucet may also not be the best choice for a smaller vanity top.

Wall-Mounted Faucet

There is one additional faucet installation type which is less common but sometimes found in older homes. A wall-mounted faucet is attached directly to the bathroom wall above the sink or freestanding basin, and it has a longer spout in order to reach the sink. Wall-mounted faucets require a separate wall-mounted valve and drain assembly. They are typically harder to find replacement faucets or repair parts for, and even when doing an affordable remodel, it may be wise to convert the plumbing to a counter or sink application.

FAUCET TECHNOLOGY

Though we won't get into how these differing faucets all function on the inside, I did want to note that not all faucets use the same mechanical technology. Most of us really don't care how our faucets work as long as we turn the handles and water comes out. However, when you have a problem with a faucet, it's nice to understand that they have different internal parts and don't all work the same way. So, let's turn our attention from the external, i.e. the four aforementioned faucet types, and look to the internal. There are four common types of faucet construction.

Compression Faucets

Compression faucets are the oldest of the four types. All compression faucets have separate handles for hot and cold water. You manually tighten and untighten these handles by rotating them to let water flow out of the faucet. Untightening the faucet handle starts the water, and tightening it again stops the water. This type of faucet is the most basic and is essentially just an on-off valve.

Ball Faucets

Ball faucets were designed to be the first washerless faucets. Unlike compression faucets, ball faucets only have one handle for both hot and cold water. They're especially common in kitchen sinks but will also find their way into the bathroom. If your faucet's handle can rotate semi-freely up and down and from side to side, then it's probably a ball faucet. The temperature, pressure, and flow rate of the water all depend on where you position the ball faucet handle.

Disc Faucets

Disc faucets are a much more recent design than either compression or ball faucets. Like ball faucets, they were designed not to rely on washers. Disc faucets are also considerably more durable than either compression or ball faucets. A disc faucet's body is much wider than other types of faucets, and it's usually cylindrical. Disc faucet handles move up and down and side to side like ball faucets, but they usually don't have as much free motion.

Cartridge Faucets

Cartridge faucets can have either one or two handles. Unlike compression faucets, however, you don't have to rotate the faucet handles to control water flow. Instead, you can simply turn a cartridge faucet handle to start the water flow. Unless there's something wrong, the handle should rotate from "off" to "on" in one smooth, easy motion. Single-handle cartridge faucets move up and down to control water flow and side-to-side to control temperature, like disc faucets. This is more than likely what you'll be buying if you're replacing your bath faucet.

FAUCET SUPPLY LINES AND SHUT-OFF VALVES

While shower faucets have their valves behind the wall and typically rely on copper or iron pipes for their water supply, sink faucets get water through supply line hoses attached to shut-off valves, also called supply-stop valves or angle stops. These are the two components needed to allow water to flow into sinks and toilets. In the case of the sink faucet, the angle stops and supply lines come out of the wall under the vanity cabinet. These valves help isolate and repair leaks near fixtures without shutting off the water supply to the entire house.

Depending on the age of the house, the existing valve may be connected to the pipe via threads, solder, or a compression fitting. I almost always replace all the angles, stops, and supply lines when doing a remodel, unless they are clearly newer and there's no sign of any issues. They are inexpensive, easy to replace, and can prevent a water leak.

SIMPLIFYING YOUR PLUMBING CHOICES

Now that I've given you way too much information on plumbing with regards to your bathroom remodel, let's simplify and decide what really makes sense for your project. In most affordable remodels, replacing the shower valve is not necessary, especially if you're not ripping out and replacing your shower walls. A replacement shower trim kit is typically what I like to use, assuming the shower faucet is working properly.

Once I've found the shower trim replacement kit or have a plan for the shower faucet, I strive to match the sink faucet to that trim. You may not be able to find an exact handle to match the shower faucet, but at least work to find the same finish and a similar style. I like all the plumbing in the room to be coordinated and look like it was thoughtfully chosen. I even like to replace the toilet handle with a matching finish and style to the sink and shower faucets.

Keep in mind that your sink faucet choices depend on the number of holes you have in your sink. If you have an existing sink that you are planning to reuse that has three holes (the four-inch widespread), you are limited to a four-inch centerset faucet or a one-hole faucet with a cover plate. If you're replacing the sink, you have the option of any of the above mentioned sink faucet choices, so be sure to think ahead and purchase the sink, faucet, and shower trim as a matching set if you can. By being aware of these small details, you will contribute to a higher quality remodel without spending any extra dollars.

CHAPTER
EIGHT

MIRRORS

A bathroom mirror might not seem like it needs that much consideration, but the type of mirror that you choose for your vanity can have a drastic impact on the overall outcome of your bathroom remodel.

There are several things to consider when choosing a bathroom mirror. There are also plenty of options. When I'm doing a remodel, I tend to select one of two options when deciding on a mirror type: frameless or framed. I typically want either a bevel or polished flat mirror that mounts on the wall directly on top of the vanity backsplash, or I want a framed mirror hung above the vanity top.

FRAMELESS

Frameless mirrors are the most common bathroom mirror and for good reason. They tend to be the least expensive option and offer a sleek style and modern appeal. This is the mirror type I have used on most of my remodels not only for the reasonable cost, but also because they make a small bathroom seem larger, offering more reflective light. Typically, the mirror should not extend beyond the edges of the bathroom vanity countertop below it, and traditionally, it's recommended the mirror be roughly two inches shorter than the vanity on both sides.

One thing to look out for when planning to use this type of mirror are obstructions. The ones I see the most are electrical outlets, which are on the wall and can get in the way of installing the mirror. Though it is possible to have a mirror shop provide a cutout for this outlet, obstructions can be tricky, and you'll want to look at all options before making any purchases.

Another thing to pay attention to is the height of the mirror. Make sure your mirror does not encroach on any light fixtures. I try to keep my mirror two or three inches below the bottom of the light fixture for a clean look.

If you decide to go the frameless route and like the size of a mirror from a big-box store, that will be your least expensive option. However, I like the look of a custom mirror cut to my exact needs, so I will usually solicit a local mirror shop to cut the mirror to my specifications. I normally have them finish the edges with a pencil polished edge (the standard type of edge with a smooth finish) over a beveled edge (an angled type of edge that gives the mirror a framed look), which saves a few bucks. I also always order an aluminum mirror channel in the same finish as my plumbing fixtures, which sits on the vanity backsplash and is attached to the wall where the new mirror will sit upon installation. This ensures the mirror will stay in place, and provides a nice, finished look.

Important note: if you're installing the mirror yourself or having a handyman attach the mirror to the wall, be sure that mirror mastic is used as the adhesive. Using anything else runs the risk of damaging the backside of the mirror, and the damage can bleed through to the front, permanently ruining the mirror.

FRAMED

Framed mirrors are among the easiest to install and change out. The mirror itself is framed in wood, metal, plastic, tile, or stone and is usually hung like a picture from hooks on the wall. Your choices are virtually limitless in style and size, especially if you have a mirror custom made. However, if using a framed mirror (or mirrors with a double sink), I generally source a finished mirror either from a big-box store or a discount home store. A framed mirror can add style and uniqueness, and it offers a custom look that will make your room a one-of-a-kind space. I will usually try to color-coordinate the mirror with the cabinet, but other times, I choose a contrasting color that will bring a little fun and character into the room.

One secret trick that I'll often do when I've decided to paint my bathroom cabinet is to purchase a mirror of my desired size and frame type, then paint the frame of the mirror to match the painted cabinet. It provides an inexpensive, customized look that gives a nice matching finishing touch.

Though I don't consider a mirrored medicine cabinet one of the main mirror options, it's probably the most common mirror found in bathrooms. My rule of thumb is that if the room already has a recessed provision for a medicine cabinet, I will either use the existing cabinet (if it's in good condition) and paint the inside, or just purchase a new one in the same size. Medicine cabinets come in all sizes and can be recessed or wall-mounted. A quality, wall-mounted medicine cabinet in the place of a wall-mounted mirror can be a good choice when there is little or no storage and it's in a size that works for you. They can be pricey, but if you need space, it can be a great option.

CHAPTER
NINE

BATHROOM
LIGHTING

Bathrooms are the place where everyone gets ready to face the world. As a result, bathroom lights are important not only for design but also function. To make sure you appear in the best light, it's important to put some thought into your bathroom lighting plan.

Lighting creates a sense of warmth and brightness that can make your house a home. Carrying that same idea into your bathroom can drastically improve this small space and provide multiple benefits when completing a budget-minded remodel.

Most smaller bathrooms generally have one light. The location of this light is typically either in the ceiling in the center of the room or above the vanity mirror. If you're lucky, you have both, or maybe even a light above the shower or tub. Regardless, addressing lighting in your remodel is a great way of adding value without a high cost. You'll be shocked at how a well-lit bathroom will improve your remodel.

VANITY LIGHT

If your existing bathroom has a vanity light—a lighting fixture above the mirror—then you can easily replace it with a new one. Large and small home improvement stores have many options to choose from, and the cost can range from $50 to $200 for a reasonably priced modern replacement. I like to install the largest light fixture that I can fit in this space to maximize the number of light bulbs. For example, if my vanity top is 36 inches wide and my mirror is 34 inches wide, then we could reasonably look to install a 24 to 30 inch light fixture.

Uplighting vs. Downlighting

When choosing the right vanity light, you may notice that some fixtures are designed for uplight, whereas others are made to shine down over the sink and countertop. Others will give you the option of simply turning the light fixture over for either uplight or downlight. Though I have used both types of lighting, I typically prefer downlighting as it puts the lighting where you need it most.

FIGURE 9.1

BEFORE

AFTER

What a difference a couple of hours makes! This vanity light was removed, taken apart, and cleaned. The light was painted, put back together, and hung back up two hours later, giving this 30-year-old *light fixture new life again. The cost was a $6.00 spray can (oil-rubbed bronze) and a few hours of DIY labor, shaving at least a couple hundred dollars off of the remodel cost.*

TYPES OF LIGHT BULBS

Light bulbs are always evolving, and technology plays a big role in the lighting we ultimately use in our homes. I would suggest doing some research on the most up-to-date efficient lighting. I generally prefer light bulbs that offer clear, bright, white light. Daylight light bulbs are a top choice for bathrooms, though some people prefer a softer white for a warmer feel. Consider whether your bathroom needs proper lighting for applying makeup or other tasks where color accuracy and appearance are important. If so, look for bathroom light bulbs that have a high CRI rating, which indicates superior color contrast and vibrancy. The higher the CRI rating, the better the bulb. Generally, a CRI of 80 or above is considered good, while a CRI of 90 or above is considered excellent.

I also routinely install a dimmer switch for bathroom lighting. Though I believe you can never have too much light in a bathroom, there are times when a dimmed room is nice, especially late at night when you don't want to wake anyone up by turning on a light.

CEILING LIGHTING

Many older homes have a single ceiling light. While this is not ideal lighting for a modern bathroom remodel, it can prove helpful for adding multiple can lighting. Adding recessed can lighting in a small bathroom is a great way to illuminate the entire room. Additionally, recessed lighting can bring a modern feel without taking up room or giving the ceiling a bulky look.

If you have an existing ceiling light, then you already have an electrical box and wiring in the ceiling. Having a licensed electrician convert that one light to multiple can lights is a relatively easy and affordable task. I also like to add lighting above the shower area, which will need to be a wet-rated fixture. If you don't have pre-existing wiring in the ceiling, you can pull wire up from the vanity light and add can lighting to the ceiling on the same switch as your vanity light.

Ultimately, I prefer both recessed can lighting and a vanity light. Bathroom lighting is important and does not have to be expensive to complete.

FIGURE 9.2

BEFORE

AFTER

The ceiling lights were gold and dated-looking, so they were removed and painted in the color oil-rubbed bronze. We achieved a new, modern look for the cost of a rattle can of paint! The gold closet door was also painted in the same color, saving over $600 on a new mirrored shower door that was an odd size and would have been a custom order.

BATHROOM FAN

Bathroom ventilation doesn't have much to do with lighting, but there is a reason I lump the two together. If you find that you need to replace your existing fan and have already hired an electrician to work on lighting, then I recommend having the fan done at the same time. This will save you some time and money, considering the electrician will already be working with the wiring in the ceiling and can simultaneously knock out both projects. Additionally, you may want to swap an old fan for a new one that includes lighting. But how do you know if you need to install a new fan or keep your old one?

Typically, bathrooms have either a window or a bathroom fan (aka a "fart fan," as remodelers typically refer to them). Some older bathrooms have both, but most bathrooms I've worked in have one or the other. If you have a window in your bathroom, but it's hard to access or you don't want to keep it open, you may want to consider adding a fan. However, installing fans can be costly and invasive, as you'll need exhaust ducting, and you'll probably want to seek the advice of a remodeling professional before you start opening up your ceiling.

If you currently have an exhaust fan in your ceiling (which is normally where they are located), you have a few options while doing your remodel. The first option is to leave the existing fan alone. If it's working properly and not too noisy, you may not need to do anything to it. The second option is to give it a small touch up. If the operation of the fan is adequate, but it does not look good, then you can remove the fan cover and simply freshen it up with a can of spray paint.

Noisy fans or broken fans should be replaced. Removing and reinstalling a new fan involves cutting drywall out and exposing the joists to properly remove the old fan and install the new one, so this is not a straightforward DIY project.

There are some choices when choosing a new fan. Fans can include a light and even a heating option, though you will need to discuss these options with your electrician, as they may require extra wiring beyond what's currently in your ceiling.

Because this book assumes a standard 5 x 9 bathroom, you won't have to worry too much about CFMs, which is the cubic feet per minute, or the measurement of airflow that the fan motor is capable of. Most small bathrooms will require a fan that provides 70-90 CFM, which is what you'll find at most big-box hardware stores. These fans should be of similar size as the one you're removing, so the fitment should be appropriate.

CHAPTER
TEN

SHOWER
DOORS

The shower door can be a complicated and expensive part of any bath remodel. Although I could probably write an entire book on the shower door alone, in this chapter, I will try to simplify the process by primarily talking about the most common type of doors found in our typical 5 x 9 bathroom.

If you Google "shower door options," you'll be amazed at the number of options. The right type of shower door for you is a decision you can make based on the type of tub/shower you have. For example, a neo-angle shower door is one type of glass shower door system, but it's only useful to know about this door if you have a neo-angle shower base, which most of us do not have, especially in a traditional 5 x 9 bathroom. As we discussed in the first chapter, not all bathrooms are the same. The shower door you choose must work and fit with the tub or shower base you have, so knowing what options are available for your remodel is an important first step.

NO SHOWER DOOR AT ALL

Since this book is about options (remember the good, better, and best scenarios), it's fitting to mention first that a shower door may not be needed or desired at all. Over the years, I have seen many bathrooms with tubs and shower enclosures that do not have any type of door on them. These enclosures typically have some sort of plastic curtain hung from a rod that keeps the water inside the shower area. Oftentimes, for a bathtub in a hall or guest bathroom that is not regularly used, a decorative fabric curtain is a nice design option. I've also seen fiberglass bathtub units that originally had glass doors installed in them removed, and the homeowner had the enclosure refinished after the shower door holes were repaired and filled. Many rental properties may also decide to no longer provide shower doors for their tenants, instead installing shower rods in an effort to minimize maintenance calls on older shower doors, which lessens cost over the long term.

TYPES OF SHOWER DOORS

Depending on the type and size of the tub/shower enclosure you have in your bathroom, there are two types of shower doors that are most common: the bypass shower door and the pivot shower door.

Bypass Shower Door

The most common type of shower door is the two-panel bypass type. This is the door type that's on almost every 5-foot bathtub or shower pan enclosure. This type of door consists of two glass panels—one inner and one outer—that hang from a header channel and roll back and forth with the ability to bypass each other, allowing entry to the front or back of the tub/shower enclosure. If you have a shower base that is less than 48 inches wide, a bypass door can not be used, as the glass panels will be too narrow to allow entry. In this case, a pivot door is an option.

Pivot or Hinged Door

When a shower enclosure is not wide enough to accept a bypass door, the pivot door is the best option. Pivot doors are typically custom ordered, unlike bypass doors, which can also be custom-made but are typically found in local hardware stores or big-box stores. This is because of the sheer number of 5-foot standard tubs that are in most bathrooms and bypass doors do not have to be fit for exact width, as there is an overlap between the two glass panes.

Pivot doors, however, need to be more exact and will need to be measured by a professional to ensure proper fitting. Pivot doors can consist of just the door itself (no other glass panel) or with a fixed panel, but there are also unlimited custom options. Because pivot doors are custom doors based on the needs of the shower they're meant to enclose, they can be customized. For example, a 42-inch shower base (too small for a bypass door) could have a 30-inch pivot door with a 12-inch inline fixed panel. The same shower could be made to have a 28-inch pivot door and a 14-inch fixed panel. Both of these examples could have the pivot door either left or right hinged or be on either the left or right side of the enclosure depending on where the plumbing is located and how much room there is for the door to swing open without any obstructions.

As a rule, if you have an opening less than 48 inches (measuring from wall to wall across the top of the tub or shower base), you should consider installing a pivot door. Shower pans up to 48 inches (roughly 46 inches measuring from wall to wall) is the minimum required to install the smallest bypass doors with enough room to get in and out of the shower. Consulting a shower door professional is a great way to learn about all of the size and design options available to you based on your specific tub or shower configuration.

SHOWER DOOR CONSTRUCTION TYPES

Regardless of whether you use a bypass door or pivot door, there are still a few decisions you'll have to make about the door you choose. There are two basic shower door construction types: framed and frameless.

Frameless Shower Doors

A frameless shower enclosure uses sturdy, tempered glass (usually ¼ inch to ½ inch thick) that does not require the support of metal around its exterior edges. The frameless shower door is considered the nicer of the two options and will typically be more expensive. The result of a frameless unit is a cleaner look with less aluminum channeling in the way, providing a more modern aesthetic that lends itself to more visibility to see what's inside the tub or shower enclosure, assuming you use clear glass. It better highlights the shower walls and plumbing fixtures which, if new, you'll want to show off!

Frameless doors are not without any aluminum structure, however. Frameless doors do generally include some metal, though effort is made to minimize the metal components except for clips on any stationary panels, hinges, and handles.

Framed Shower Doors

Considerably less spendy, framed shower doors are a nice option, especially for a lower-budget remodel. The reason the framed door costs less than the frameless—even though there's more metal used—is typically the glass thickness. Because framed doors have the metal structure to support and protect them, the glass can be thinner, which brings down both the cost and weight.

Framed shower door glass panels are typically 3/16 of an inch, making them the cheaper option. However, just because they're less expensive than the frameless option doesn't mean they're short on style. Framed shower doors can add an excellent look to your remodel by matching the color of the aluminum frame to your bathroom fixtures, especially if you've chosen a non-traditional plumbing finish. For example, an oil-rubbed, bronze, framed shower door paired with the same bronze plumbing can really make a statement. Additionally, when you don't want clear glass and opt for some privacy glass, the framed unit can be the better option.

FIGURE 10.1

BEFORE

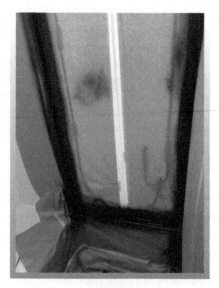

DURING

AFTER

This 1990s cultured marble walk-in steam shower was given a low-cost makeover, which included painting the existing framed gold shower doors (two oil-rubbed bronze spray cans), replacing the plumbing trim, and adding a marble seat directly on top of the existing cultured marble seat. Even the shower drain was painted to match. Notice that ¼" drywall was installed over the dated wood wall and 12'x12' peel and stick linoleum flooring was installed directly over the old linoleum. Amazing! Had the entire shower been replaced, the cost was quoted in excess of $5,000 and would have taken 2-3 weeks. The mini makeover option took just three days and came in at a cost of $1,650.

SHOWER DOOR GLASS OPTIONS

Most frameless shower doors use clear glass. The thick, heavy glass has a solid feel and is definitely an upgrade. Framed doors can also go well with clear glass, especially if you want to highlight what's on the other side. However, there are downsides to clear glass, and there are other options.

Clear Glass

At their best, clear glass shower doors can make a shower enclosure inviting and glamorous, but if clear glass is your choice, regardless of your frame option, be prepared for some daily maintenance. Depending on the water conditioning in your house, water spots will need to be squeegeed after each use to maintain that clean, clear glass appearance. Clear glass that is not regularly maintained could be stained with hard water spots that may not be removable and can permanently damage the glass. However, if you're willing to put in a little time and elbow grease and do the required work on your clear glass, you'll have an enclosure that will look new for many years.

Obscured Glass

Any glass option other than clear glass is called obscured glass. Obscured glass is any type of glass that adds obscurity, privacy, or design to the glass. This includes frosted, etched, colored, or any other type of glass with texture. The options for obscured glass are limitless, and though basic obscured textured or rain glass is typically less expensive than clear glass, most other obscured choices will add cost to your shower door.

In the 90s, when I was selling shower doors as a bath remodeler, I sold thousands of shower doors, and many of my clients chose custom designs. Though many of those doors were works of art, I've always thought that if your remodeling project is going to stand the test of time, clear glass or traditional obscured glass are the best options and will never go out of style. Tasteful frosted or textured glass adds privacy and a bit of fun to your shower, and they're easier to maintain than clear glass. Although I prefer clear glass even with the added maintenance, I've used obscured glass many times in my remodels to help hide shower walls that weren't as new as I would have liked. An obscured shower door can be the first thing people see when walking into your bathroom, and it can cover an older bathtub or shower enclosure to pull off a clean look.

CHAPTER
ELEVEN

TOILETS

It seems fitting to save the toilet for one of the last chapters of the book, as it's typically the last fixture installed in a bathroom remodel. The toilet is easily one of the most used fixtures in any bathroom, so it's worth spending some time discussing it. Although you may come into this chapter thinking that there's not much involved with toilets, there's more information than you might think, and there are choices to be made when replacing the toilet.

For this book, I will not get into specialty toilets with additions like bidets and seat-cleaning gadgets, but rather the standard toilets that are seen in almost every bathroom remodel, no matter the room size. For your remodel, you may be able to use your existing toilet if you just give it a good cleaning and change the seat, which will save you some money.

Fortunately, toilets have come a long way over the years, now offering numerous types, designs, functions, and flushing capabilities. The most common type of toilet is the two-piece toilet (as opposed to a one-piece), which is the one we will primarily focus on for your remodel. It's the toilet you more than likely have in your bathroom and the one I would recommend should you decide to replace it. Two-piece toilets are ideal for adults since the seat is higher than a one-piece toilet. While one-piece toilets are a bit more expensive, they are more durable. One-piece toilets may make sense for very small bathrooms because they take up less space. They are especially useful when you are looking for a sleek or specific design.

There are also several flush options for toilets today. Older homes almost exclusively had gravity-fed flush systems. Push the handle down, and water forces the contents in the bowl down the waste pipeline with gravity. Even if you're replacing an older toilet, you'll have a few choices, and you'll be able to choose from some added efficiencies that are now available.

DUAL-FLUSH TECHNOLOGY

On a dual-flush toilet, a type of gravity-fed toilet, the flushing handle on the side is not present. Instead, two buttons on the top of the tank let you select a partial flush for liquid waste or a full flush for solid waste. The best models effectively flush solid waste in their full-flush mode and leave no trace of liquid waste in partial-flush mode. Other dual-flush models lack power, so you could end up having to flush twice. If this is of interest to you for your remodel, do your research and check reviews of your options, as technology for toilets is constantly changing.

POWER FLUSH TOILETS

There are plenty of positive things to say about power flush, or pressure-assisted, toilets. Their brawny flushing action is water-efficient, helps keep the bowl clean, and virtually eliminates clogs. But that high-octane power comes at a cost, and not just a financial one: some pressure-assisted toilets sound like jet engines as they forcefully perform their jobs. Though the benefits of a power flush toilet may be appealing, you may not appreciate the sound of it in the middle of night when you wake up your spouse.

TOILET OPTIONS (GOOD, BETTER, AND BEST SCENARIOS)

You have a few options regarding the toilet while doing a remodel. If the toilet is in good condition, works properly, and is in the location you want, you can reuse it and not spend any of your remodeling budget on the toilet other than changing the seat. If you're happy with the toilet but it doesn't flush well, consider purchasing an inexpensive rebuild kit, which typically includes replacement parts for all of the working equipment in a toilet tank. Using a kit is an easy way to save money and make the toilet virtually new again without replacing the entire fixture.

Conversely, if you plan to replace it with a new toilet in the same location, it's generally an easy swap, and most remodeling projects do not require a toilet relocation. Regardless of if you're replacing the toilet or not, maybe you want to move the toilet to a new location. If toilet relocation is a consideration for your remodeling project, then it will get more complicated and costly, especially with a concrete slab foundation. If you have a slab foundation, moving the toilet can't be done without some major demolition, and I would not recommend this for an affordable remodel. If your home is on a raised foundation that has a crawl space, you can reconfigure the bathroom and move the toilet to a new location that may be better for what you're trying to achieve.

FIGURE 11.1

BEFORE

AFTER

This bathroom was a disaster! And yes, it could have been saved and made to look new again for a few thousand dollars. However, the bathroom had a poor layout, and we wanted to move the toilet and vanity to make for a better flowing room. The entire bathroom was gutted and completely remodeled. A new porcelain on steel bathtub was installed with a new shower valve and 12 x 12 granite tiles installed as wet wall all the way up to the ceiling (a window was also added in the shower). The vanity cabinet was purchased in a box, assembled, and installed under a prefabricated granite countertop with an undermount sink. An 8" widespread faucet was installed to match the shower plumbing. A new mirror and light fixture were installed as well as a new elongated dual flush toilet. 16 x 16 travertine tile was installed on the floor, and a nice soft yellow paint color was chosen to finish the room. The remodeling time was roughly 2.5 weeks at a total cost of $8,500.

ELONGATED VS. ROUND

We'll assume that in your standard 5 x 9 bathroom, you're going to be working within the confines of what you have and not moving the toilet. We'll also assume that because toilets are not a large chunk of your remodeling budget, you'll be replacing the existing toilet. Therefore, you'll need to decide not only the type of flush technology, but also the bowl configuration, which is either elongated or round.

The difference between the two choices comes down to the shape of the bowl. There's the elongated shape, which is more of an oval bowl, and there's a round shape, which is a shorter, rounder bowl. The choice really comes down to space, and generally, the elongated shape is the preferred toilet.

However, there are times when the elongated bowl won't work, and the round bowl is the only option. This usually occurs when you have a tight space around the toilet and there's a bathroom or shower door that could swing in front of the toilet bowl. In this case, you'll want to use the round bowl, because you don't have the extra few inches needed that an elongated bowl requires. However, if space allows, I would recommend an elongated toilet, and one that is the tallest you can fit, as there are also height options.

Taller toilets are generally better for older people, tall people, and people with mobility issues. Most people would appreciate the few extra inches provided with a taller toilet.

The taller the toilet, the taller the tank. If you have a banjo arm connected to your countertop (a small piece of the counter that hangs over the toilet tank; see Figure 12.1), you'll need to account for a few extra inches of space to lift off the toilet tank lid in order to service it. Most vanity tops these days don't have a banjo arm, so if you have a standard countertop without any obstructions, you can have any height you prefer.

If you have a countertop with a banjo arm, then a taller toilet might not work for your particular remodel, so pay attention to the tank height dimensions before you purchase.

One thing that I've found over the years is that as much as I try to save fixtures whenever I can, sometimes, replacing the toilet is the smart move. Even on a shoestring budget, toilets are inexpensive compared to most other new fixtures. When you buy a new toilet, it comes with a wax ring, a new seat, and a brand-new tank, and you're all but guaranteed not to have any leaks or issues with it. If you try to rebuild or clean up an old toilet, there's labor involved, so there's the potential for the cost to be equal to or possibly even exceed just buying a new one.

TOILET HARDWARE

One detail that I often see overlooked, even in higher-end remodels, is to match the toilet handle with the other plumbing in the room. Gravity-flush toilets typically come with an installed, generic chrome handle unless you opt for the dual-flush toilet. However, if your toilet does come with a handle, spend the extra time and money to match the toilet handle with the handles on your vanity and shower plumbing. Most people overlook this small detail that can really add value to your remodel. It's a nice, custom touch that costs very little.

CHAPTER
TWELVE

FLOORING

I've chosen flooring as one of the last chapters in this book because it's typically one of the last big items to be installed in a complete bathroom remodel. Like shower walls and vanity tops, flooring options are virtually endless. Flooring finishes and designs can be overwhelming, but in this chapter—assuming that you're going to replace the floor and not keep the existing one—I'll make it easier for you by narrowing down some options that are sure to please. Before we get into some of the secrets of this area of your remodel, though, let's first dive into some of the most common flooring choices.

NATURAL STONE

Slate, marble, limestone, travertine, granite, and sandstone, each with slightly different properties and looks, are all common, natural stone products that are popular choices for bathroom flooring. These products are durable, scratch-resistant, and will help increase the resale value of your home more than other flooring choices, though it's also the most expensive option. Stone flooring is naturally water-resistant and will last a long time. However, it is hard and cold, which can be slippery and uncomfortable underfoot, so keep this in mind if you choose natural stone.

TILE

Probably the most popular choice for bathroom flooring is tile. There are two primary types of tiles to choose from—ceramic and porcelain. The difference between porcelain and ceramic tile comes down to water absorption rate, with porcelain boasting a lower water absorption rate (and usually a higher cost). Porcelain is also slightly harder than ceramic tile. However, unlike natural stone, tile options are endless, and they're a good choice for their durability and water resistance as well. Tile offers a wide range of prices, styles, colors, and patterns. Even after you choose your tile, there are more customization options based on how you choose to lay the pattern.

VINYL

Vinyl flooring is incredibly resilient which is why it's often used in heavy-traffic areas like hospitals, grocery stores, and of course, bathrooms. Vinyl was one of the most commonly used floor types from the 1950s to 1970s and has long been the most popular hard-surface flooring in the United States. Vinyl is one of the lowest cost options and is a great choice for small bathrooms because it's customizable.

If you're considering vinyl for your remodel, there are a few different kinds to be familiar with: sheet, plank, and tile. The biggest benefit of sheet vinyl is that it's cut in one piece and installed without any seams, making for simple installation. Pick your pattern, and it's a quick and easy glue-down installation that any professional installer will be able to complete in just an hour or two.

Vinyl plank and vinyl tile flooring have become great choices in recent years as well, as manufacturers are creating attractive flooring that's still very affordable and, like sheet vinyl flooring, quick and easy to install. Additionally, this type of flooring offers styles that look like stone or wood and can leave your small bathroom looking like a high-end remodel for a fraction of the cost and effort.

Vinyl flooring is waterproof, durable, and typically will not scratch. One of the things I like best about vinyl is that if you have an existing vinyl floor that is in good shape, but you're looking for an upgrade, a new vinyl floor can oftentimes be installed directly on top of the old floor, eliminating the cost and time of tearing out and hauling away the old floor.

Now that we've shared some viable bathroom flooring options, it's also worthwhile to go over a few flooring options that are not ideal for bathrooms.

FLOORING THAT IS NOT RECOMMENDED FOR THE BATHROOM

Real Wood Flooring

Hardwood is a beautiful flooring option, but it rarely has a place in the bathroom or any other room where water is frequently used. Hardwood is not waterproof and is highly susceptible to water damage. If even a small amount of water makes its way into the core of hardwood planks, it can rot the wood from the inside out. Do yourself a favor and stay away from hardwood in the bathroom, especially when there are great products made from tile and vinyl that are made to look like wood.

Carpet

I remember having a carpeted bathroom as a kid. I also remember having wall-to-wall shag carpet everywhere else!

We all know the feeling of tiptoeing across a cold bathroom floor, but the solution to getting around this discomfort is not installing carpet in your bathroom. Carpet soaks up water, so if you place it in a room with constant moisture, you are setting yourself up for disaster. If a cold bathroom floor is something that you just can't live with, ask your contractor about installing heated flooring. There may be options that can give you the comfort you're looking for with the right flooring choice.

Laminate Flooring

Laminate flooring is great if you want the look and feel of real wood without the expense, but just like real wood, it's not a good choice for bathrooms. Laminate is made from the layering of a number of different synthetic fabrics, usually resin and fiberboard materials underneath a wood photographic applique with a clear protective layer on top that allows the wood visual to show through. Though laminate is water-resistant, it is not waterproof, so if it gets wet, it can leave you with problems in the long run, including water damage and even mold or mildew issues if left untreated.

ADDING VALUE TO YOUR FLOORING CHOICE

We've looked at the three main types of flooring that are available and recommended. We've also gone over three more that are not recommended. And maybe you'll decide to keep your existing floor in action a little longer and spend your budget dollars in other parts of the bathroom. Whatever your choice, I wanted to provide a few thoughts (and secrets!) on bathroom flooring.

If You Have Existing Tile or Stone Floors

I've tackled old tile floors in bathroom projects many times. Though flooring does not have a "good," "better," or "best" option, there are some things to keep in mind if you have an existing tile floor that you're considering replacing.

Let's first start with what's underneath the old tile floor. Tile and stone installations are properly installed in one of two scenarios, and that typically depends on the type of construction of your house. Your house was either built on a concrete slab foundation, or it was built using a raised foundation method. The reason I bring this up now is that the flooring that's currently installed—as well as any new flooring—will differ depending on your home's subfloor.

If it's on a slab foundation, you likely have concrete under the existing tile, and that tile was installed with mortar directly on top of the concrete.

If you're on a raised foundation (or on a second story), you probably have a plywood subfloor, thereby needing an additional step in the installation process. This additional step involves installing concrete sheets on top of the plywood subfloor for the new tile or stone to properly adhere to. Some of the brand names of this product are HardieBacker or Wonderboard, among others. They all are screwed and/or glued to existing plywood to ensure a solid subfloor that's water-resistant and will provide a better bond when using mortar.

When replacing your existing tile or stone floor, the demolition process will differ depending on which type of subfloor you have, and that can add to the time, cost, and mess of installing a new floor.

Shortcuts to a Beautiful New Floor

Refinishing your existing floor can be an option. If your existing tile floor is in good structural condition, you may be able to change the color of the floor by refinishing the tile and grout. A refinishing company may be able to completely transform the old tile into a new look without having to remove it and potentially open up a can of worms. This tends to work best with smaller tiles, like mosaic, and can be a good option for the low price point.

However, I think the best way to cover an old tile or stone floor—assuming you have the option not to tear it out—is to lay new tile or stone directly over the old floor. This is a home flipping trick that I have done many, many times over the decades. The results come out stunning, and it's the installation method that I prefer when possible. As I mentioned in the shower wall chapter, I've been installing new tile or stone over old tile shower walls for years with excellent results. The old tile will need to be chemically cleaned, and I like to grind the shine off of the old tile for adhesion but prep involved with this type of installation is minimal should it be an option for your remodel.

Regardless of the installation method, if you're going with new tile or stone for your project, here are a few more tips.

Buy What You Love, Even If It's Expensive!

Now, I know what you're thinking. Up to this point, I've been trying to save you money and keep you on a budget, and now I'm telling you to go for it? That's right—I am.

We are working with a 5 x 9 bathroom, which is only 45 square feet. Even if you're looking at a tile or stone selection that's a few bucks more, the overall material cost is minimal compared to other bathroom fixtures. If the tile choice you love is, say, $3 more per square foot, that's less than $150 dollars more for the floor you really want. Besides, let's face it—bathroom flooring is an important part of the remodel, so you should get what you want.

The installation cost of the material will not change whether the tile is $2 per square foot or $7 per square foot. The process is exactly the same.

Size Does Matter

I've found over the years that, when working in small spaces, your intuition might tell you to use smaller tiles. However, I would recommend doing just the opposite. Using larger tiles for a small bathroom floor can provide the illusion of space and counteract that claustrophobic feeling present in smaller rooms, giving it a sense of openness and a less cluttered feeling.

One other advantage to using larger tiles is that it minimizes the amount of grout lines present in the room, reducing maintenance. Let's face it: grout is the toughest part of a tile floor to clean, so fewer grout lines means less cleaning and less grout sealing over the years.

FIGURE 12.1

BEFORE

AFTER

Here is an example of new ceramic tile floors being installed over the existing pink and purple tile. Other remodeling in the room includes the vanity top being repurposed and refinished with a multicolor granite-like finish as discussed in Chapter 5. The bathroom was repainted, and the round toilet was replaced with a new elongated one. As we detailed in Chapter 2, the bathtub was refinished, and new tub plumbing trim was installed. Notice that the vanity faucet was replaced and matches the new tub plumbing, but the sink was not replaced nor was the cabinet; only the knobs were added. The mirror was replaced with a larger mirror that extends the full length of the counter, which helps make the room feel larger and brighter. The light fixture was replaced, and matching towel bars and a toilet paper holder were also installed for the finishing touches. A shower curtain was chosen instead of installing a new shower door. Using many of the secret tricks outlined in this book, the total cost of this remodel was just over $3,000 and took roughly one week.

Creative Color and Installation Patterns

Even if you don't select an expensive tile, you'd be amazed by what a tile setter can do with a nontraditional installation pattern. Being creative with the pattern and color of your tile can give the room a custom feel and add fun to a small space. Graphic tiles are another way to add uniqueness to your remodel and allow you to be creative in a small space.

I like using a diagonal pattern instead of a plain, straight tile install. Another option is using multiple colors and creating a small border around the room with a diagonal pattern in between. Though I tend to remodel with neutral colors, taking a chance on a bold color can create a focal point and make a room that's all your own.

CHAPTER THIRTEEN

ACCESSORIES

Your bathroom remodel will be incomplete without the proper accessories and finishing touches, including towel bars, toilet paper holders, and robe hooks. Small bathrooms leave little wall space for all of these critical comforts, so spend some time mapping out what's important to you, who will be using the room, and how they'll be using it.

I've found that because wall space is at a premium in a 5 x 9 bathroom, you'll be lucky to get more than one large towel bar installed. I like to install as many hooks as possible to ensure that everyone who regularly uses the room has a place to hang a towel. The bathroom door is a great place to hang multiple hooks. You can even get creative by installing a wood-backed, multiple-hook plate on the door rather than installing multiple single hooks throughout the room into drywall that typically won't hold up over time.

If you've opted for new plumbing fixtures in the shower and sink areas of your bathroom, be mindful that there are probably matching accessories for the line. This is a great way to tie in all of your selections with similar handles and finish designs, and it will leave your remodel with professional-looking results.

EPILOGUE

I first entered the bathroom remodeling and refinishing business at age 24 with a degree in business management and work experience in a body shop. Three good friends and I started a bathtub refinishing business and learned the industry the hard way. Well, it wasn't really the hard way at the time—it was the only way. Cell phones and the Internet didn't exist. We had to go door to door teaching people about refinishing, an option many people hadn't heard of.

A lot of times, the property managers and owners I talked to didn't believe I could refinish their bathtubs and would turn me away. Oftentimes before I left, I'd make an offer. "Let me do a tub for you, free of charge," I'd tell them. "If you like what I do, then you can pay me for the next one." That's how we got our first clients. Now, my company Commercial Bath Refinishing is one of the largest bathtub refinishing companies in the U.S., and not only have we nailed down the refinishing process, but we can now do our jobs while also being eco-conscious.

Every time we refinish a bathtub, what we're really doing is preventing the same tub from ending up in a landfill. We take care to save any materials we can instead of throwing them away, whether that means finding a way to repurpose them in the space we're remodeling or donating them to a charitable cause like Habitat for Humanity. Not only is proper waste removal the legal thing to do, it's also the right thing to do. Commercial Bath Refinishing knows that doing the right thing has brought us success for over thirty years, and it will continue bringing us success for years to come.

THE SECRETS DON'T CHANGE

Through my decades of experience, I've realized one key fact about the bathroom remodeling industry: no matter how much time passes, the work stays the same. Styles and preferences change, but the core function of a bathroom does not. The way a lightbulb looks or works may improve, but at the end of the day, we still use it to light up a room no matter how advanced it is. The same is true for a number of fixtures I encounter every day: toilets, showers, baths, mirrors, and more. This means even when times change and prices fluctuate, anyone will still be able to use the tips I've included in this book. This information was true thirty years ago and will be true ten, twenty, thirty years from now.

No matter how much time passes, bathroom remodeling and refinishing will never be a glamorous or glitzy profession. It's not as complicated as brain surgery or as essential as firefighting. Despite that, I love what I do, so much so that I sometimes work seven days a week.

My day is different every day. There's always a new project, opportunity, or problem to tackle. My work doesn't feel like work when I have the privilege of helping clients take something old and make it new again. As you've read, I can even blend old and new together in many cases, preserving the history of a place while still making it modern, functional, and appealing. Plus, helping people transform their spaces into phenomenal rooms they can be proud of—all while maintaining their budget—has always been gratifying to me.

When you think about it, the bathroom is the first room we visit when we wake up and the last room we visit before we go to bed. It's an important space we all spend a lot of time in. Why not invest some time to create an oasis in your own home, or at the very least, fix some blemishes here and there to improve your bathroom's overall appearance? After reading this book, I hope you have taken away enough helpful information to start or finish such a project. I will have been successful if you close this book and feel better prepared to purchase the proper supplies, talk to your contractor, and build the bathroom you're envisioning. Most of all, I hope you recognize how remodeling a bathroom on a budget is possible with the right decisions and a few tricks of the trade. If you've read the book this far and finally have the motivation to complete your bathroom remodel, then I've done my job.

NOTES

1. Yun, Lawrence et al., "2022 Remodeling Impact Report," April 2022, https://cdn.nar.realtor/sites/default/files/documents/2022-remodeling-impact-report-04-19-2022.pdf.

2. "2022 Cost vs Value Report," Remodeling, accessed October 11, 2022, https://www.remodeling.hw.net/cost-vs-value/2022/.

3. "Cost to Remodel a Bathroom in 2022," HomeAdvisor, June 2, 2022, https://www.homeadvisor.com/cost/bathrooms/remodel-a-bathroom/.

4. Tom Sightings, "5 Home Renovations That Pay Off (and 2 That Don't)," January 24, 2017, https://realestate.usnews.com/real-estate/articles/home-renovations-that-pay-off-and-that-dont.

5. "Polymer," Madehow, accessed October 11, 2022, http://www.madehow.com/knowledge/Polymer.html.

6. "Bathtub Installation & Replacements Costs in 2022," HomeAdvisor, June 14, 2022, https://www.homeadvisor.com/cost/plumbing/install-a-bathtub/.

7. Henry Parker, "The Pros and Cons of Travertine Tile," accessed October 11, 2022, https://homereference.net/travertine-tile-pros-cons/.

Made in United States
Orlando, FL
11 November 2024